One Last Scherzo

poems by

Margaret Chula

Finishing Line Press
Georgetown, Kentucky

One Last Scherzo

"*Music gives a soul to the universe, wings to the mind, flight to the imagination, and life to everything.*" —Plato

"*Music is the shorthand of emotion.*" —Leo Tolstoy

Copyright © 2020 by Margaret Chula
ISBN 978-1-64662-243-6 First Edition
All rights reserved under International and Pan-American Copyright Conventions. No part of this book may be reproduced in any manner whatsoever without written permission from the publisher, except in the case of brief quotations embodied in critical articles and reviews.

ACKNOWLEDGMENTS

I am grateful to Andrea Hollander, Donna Prinzmetal, and Penelope Scambly Schott for reading and commenting on poems in earlier versions of the manuscript.

Great thanks to Playa at Summer Lake, Oregon, for a 2018 residency, which offered a serene space and the necessary solitude to focus on writing and revision.

And, lastly, I am indebted to the following quartets and musical ensembles who, through their evocative and performances of both new and classical music, made this project a challenging and joyful experience:

Altenberg Quartet, Brooklyn Rider, Calder Quartet, Czech Nonet, Ebène Quartet, Ensō Quartet, Jerusalem Quartet, Kronos Quartet, Mallet Quartet, Pacifica Quartet, Parker Quartet, Rastrelli Cello Quartet, Red Priest, Shanghai Quartet, Sō Percussion, Takács Quartet, Tapestry, Time for Three, Tokyo Quartet, Trio con Brio Copenhagen

Publisher: Leah Maines
Editor: Christen Kincaid
Cover Art: Stefan Fiedorowicz, www.saatchionline.com/stefanfied
Author Photo: Marq Sutherland
Cover Design: Elizabeth Maines McCleavy

Order online: www.finishinglinepress.com
also available on amazon.com

Author inquiries and mail orders:
Finishing Line Press
P. O. Box 1626
Georgetown, Kentucky 40324
U. S. A.

Table of Contents

Preface ix
Rendezvous 1
A Garret in Krakow 2
To My Muse 3
Breaking Away 4
Vienna Salon 5
Down From the Mountain 6
For Fanny 7
Retreat at Ivanovo 8
Interlude 9
Inundation 10
Out of the Blue 11
Concave 12
The Game 13
Flight 14
Sustenance 16
Purge 17
Mesto 19
Street Talk 21
Bent 22
Death is a Butterfly 24
An Argentine Gaucho 25
The Offering 26
Escapades 27
Sounds From a Yao Village 28
I Want To Live My Life in a Rothko Painting 29
Great Aunt Regina of Lyski 30
One Last Scherzo 31
Notes 32

Preface

In the summer of 2010, I received a phone call from Pat Zagelow, Executive Director of Friends of Chamber Music in Portland, Oregon.

"I have an idea I'd like to run by you," she began. "One of our patrons told me that Wimbledon has a poet laureate who composes poems while watching tennis matches. Isn't that amazing? I'm intrigued by this idea and think that poetry and music would be a much better match (no pun intended)."

A few months later, I began my three-year tenure as poet laureate of Friends of Chamber Music. Pat reserved a seat for me in the back row of Lincoln Hall at Portland State University where the concerts were held. This minimalized the distraction and disturbance both to myself and to other attendees. Before the concert began, I read the program notes to learn more about the background and time period of the composer. My pocket-sized notebook, pen, and a small flashlight were at the ready. It was a challenge to find a flashlight that afforded enough light without disturbing anyone. I tested a number of them, but they were all too bright. In the end, my husband covered the end of a mini flashlight with white cloth and fastened it on with a rubber band.

Once the concert began, I closed my eyes and shut out everything but the music. I focused on sounds, rhythms, and the interplay among the musicians. Often entire scenes would emerge in my mind, sometimes inspired by the historical background of the piece—the era, place, or circumstances in the composer's life. At other times, poems emerged from emotions evoked by the music itself.

At home, I typed up my impressions. As I edited, I allowed each poem to take on its own form. For an *avant garde* piece, like Philip Glass's "Bent", I numbered each of the eight stanzas to reflect his eight movements. The poem's short lines tumble down the page in couplets and tercets. In "An Argentine Gaucho", the visual arrangement of indented lines is meant to suggest movement—a bullfight or dancing the malambo.

One of the greatest rewards of being Poet Laureate for FOCM was meeting renowned composers and musicians. It was a pleasure to sit next to Tomas Svoboda for the debut of his *Summer Trio* performed by the Czech Nonet and to attend after-concert receptions with members of the Takács and Jerusalem Quartets.

I am grateful to Pat Zagelow for inviting me to be Poet Laureate and to all the FOCM staff and board members for offering me an opportunity to expand my imagination through writing poems inspired by music.

RENDEZVOUS[1]

They stroll side by side through a dark glade
of forest and ferns, hands close but not
touching. Moss pads their footsteps.

Here is the stream still meandering
at the same pace, as if no time had passed
since they last met.

Here is the couple. The man's mustache
frosted with gray, fasteners on his waistcoat
half undone. His cane marks their passage.

Here is the embankment where they played
as children, their small round bodies leaving
indentations, like the imprints of dozing deer.

At the edge of the stream, the woman removes
her gloves, nudges off her shoes, and rolls
down her silk stockings.

Lifting the hem of her white dress,
she enters the water, holding an umbrella
in her left hand. The man looks on.

Here is the moment when blue skies
and ebbing waves of summer
funnel into a single afternoon.

Johannes Brahms (1833-1897), String Sextet in B-flat Major, Op. 18

A GARRET IN KRAKOW[2]

Yellow birch leaves swirl and fall
like butterflies in the town square.

Cobblestones darken, splattered
with late autumn rain.

In the marketplace,
a frenzy of footsteps.

Farmers carry bins of potatoes
with tumorous eyes.

Behind closed shutters,
the poet drinks mead
to soothe his raw throat.

A cockroach scuttles
behind paper-thin walls.
Rafters squeak.

A timorous voice
that will never reach paper
huddles in a dark corner.

Penderecki, Quartet No. 3, "Leaves from an Unwritten Diary"

TO MY MUSE[3]

A flurry of clouds on a summer afternoon
and you appear in crinoline and lace

your bodice strung tight as my bow strings—
like inspiration before it ripples into music.

Come sit beside me, your exhalations
light and cool on my neck.

Do not be distracted by the resin pitch
on my bow, the stench of cabbage

boiling in the kitchen, the howl
at the back of my throat.

Tell me, will you whisper into my ear
or tear up my sheet music

with your tiny, restless hands?

Leos Janácek (1854-1928), Quartet No. 2 "Intimate Letters"
Janácek called the movements of this quartet "love letters".

BREAKING AWAY[4]

Finally alone in Vienna not having to share
the parlor with my father. It's springtime.
Catkins dangle from new green leaves.
Genteel women pass by in pastel bonnets,
umbrellas loosely furled, ready for sunshine or rain.

The strings of my violin sing more sweetly
in solitude. No longer Leopold's cub,
I've escaped from the confines of his love.
All those years of restraint and obedience.

My arms hang loosely by my side
as I saunter down the avenue.
My heart, too, feels light.
Even my bow hairs no longer break with tension.
The metallic taste is gone from my mouth.

Now and then, I imagine Papa pacing at night
across the worn carpet in our Salzburg parlor
candle burning low as he sits at his desk,
dips his quill into the inkwell, and writes
Come home, dear boy, come home.

Wolfgang Amadeus Mozart, Quartet in D Major, K. 499 "Hoffmeister"

VIENNA SALON[5]

The gentry arrive, stomping snow from fur-lined boots.
Ladies flaunt loosely-wound chignons, held together
by hairpins dusted with snow that melts in the heat

of the fireplace. They take seats of honor in velvet
chairs that welcome the flounce of taffeta,
the rustle of luxury they married into.

Straight-backed chairs for the gentlemen. Feet flat
on the floor, grounding them to their position in life:
the privileged elite with an appreciation for music.

The composer sits alone in the farthest corner,
bundled in a woolen coat that smells of mildew.
His music bathes the guests in sweet melody.

Soaring notes of the first violin. A cello, soothing
as mulled wine. Viola, sensuous and sedate.
And the humble second violin reminding us

that we each have our place.

Ludwig van Beethoven, Quartet in G Major, Op. 18, No. 2

DOWN FROM THE MOUNTAIN

Dressed in black, mantled in snow
the quartet descends the mountain.
The first violinist's top glitters
in the frost—crystals illuminated
by the sun. Her skirt sashays in ruffles,
black as the moraine is white.

All four hold hands, skipping down
the slope in unison. The men's tailcoats
flap like ravens' wings. The woman's
spike heels leave pinpricks in the snow.
Their confidence is contagious.

They have returned from a pilgrimage:
seeking advice from their musical guru,
Meister Mendelssohn, who sits alone
on a hillock playing his violin with an icicle.
When it melts, he warms his fingers
inside his waistcoat.

Soon he will come down from the mountain
and join them in town for a steaming mug
of hot cocoa.

Felix Mendelssohn (1809-1847), Quartet in E-flat Major, Op 12

FOR FANNY[6]
(on the death of Mendelssohn's sister)

Rose petals open slowly,
tentative bloom of the timid

like your soft-petaled skin
released fragrance

the air hesitating
then accepting

then dissipating
like notes blown inside

a whirlwind that ends
in a dark tunnel.

Your fragrance
reached no one but me

wrapped in a cocoon,
an adagio of adieu.

Your flower garden, now
overcome with brambles

and weeds without a name
and you, beneath the soil,

still nourishing.

Felix Mendelssohn (1809-1847), Quartet in F minor, Op. 80

RETREAT AT IVANOVO

Ghosts join me at the table—clink their empty glasses.
Their features are blurred, eye sockets empty of things
remembered or imagined.

Fear swirls her black cloak among them
like a plague that has surfaced, dank
and rancid, from the Uvod River.

Cigarette smoke spirals to the ceiling. Musical notes
trail upward in bars and clefs to the roosting racks
where chickens once slept.

A fly batters its wings against the window
even though the door is wide open.
Frantic drone of its ebbing life.

Now the composers' ghosts have curled up
inside their vodka glasses. The fly lies dead on the sill.
Finally, I am alone.

Dmitri Shostakovich, String Quartet No. 2 in A Major, Op. 68 (1944)

INTERLUDE[7]

Descending steps to the basement,
it's darkness I seek—my heart sealed
like red wine laid down in a cellar
to mature with the waiting.

Stone steps, cold and merciless.
Glimmer of light from a window.
Coal smell. Mold, too, has sought
refuge inside these hoary walls.

I recline on a settee
patterned with paisley.
Tucked between the cushions,
a sprinkling of smelling salts.

From upstairs, the sound of laughter
recalls years with my brother—
how we'd sit side by side
tuning up to play our evensong.

Ludwig van Beethoven's Quartet in F minor, Op. 95 "Serioso"

INUNDATION[8]

The earth hums, squeaks, groans.
   A young boy practices his violin,
      notes flat and resigned.

Preschoolers take out their blankets for a nap.
   A waitress dips her hands in soapy water.
      Farmers work the soil before flooding their rice fields.
         Two friends drink green tea and gossip.

For some, these are their last moments.

Another rumble. A factory siren.
   A dog howls, then lurches
      like a drunkard on uneven ground.

Asphalt cracks. Buildings sway. Dishes crash.
   Tractors tip. Power lines tangle and rip.
      Computer screens go dark. Office girls scream.

Hokusai's wave rushes towards them
   swallowing boats, tiny fishermen,
      trucks, houses—everything, everyone.

There must be some way out of here.

But there is no here left, no uphill exit
   from the gullet of the wave grinding
      its teeth on timber and power lines.

No way out.

Jacob ter Veldhuis (1951 -), Quartet No 3 "There must be some way out of here"

OUT OF THE BLUE[9]

A woman is holding
the curved shoulder bone
of her husband.

Just this bone.

Is this the shoulder bone
she rested her head on
when they hugged good-bye
that blue-sky September morning?

What to do with the bone?

Smooth as his cheek after he shaved.
   Caress it.

Smoky as his hair from the campfire.
   Inhale it.

Imagine it
   with taut muscles and skin.

Place the bone to your ear.
   Listen for his exhalation.

Steve Reich (1936 -), WTC (World Trade Center) 9/11

CONCAVE

Shape of the violist curving
into sound, rising and exhaling.

Arc of a fingernail discarded
on a beach among shards of shells.

Sheared-off end of a parenthesis, no longer
holding up its end of the afterthought.

The aftermath of a farmer's life, walking
humpbacked through a field of poppies.

A mother sheltering her sick child,
eyes glazed with lethargy.

Phases of the moon
from waxing to waning

their shapes back to back
like an old couple

curled away from each other
in winter sleep.

Johannes Brahms, Quintet in F Major, Op. 88

THE GAME

My heartbeat quickens
as I hide in the hollow
of a tree, scrunched up
like a small toad,
knees to chest.

Spider webs
tickle my nose.
Sweat trickles
down my eyelids.
Braids stick to
the back of my neck.

I watch as light
changes on the field,
listen to birds
sing their vespers.

Feet numb,
hands tingling,
I wait in vain
for *Allee-allee-in-free.*

It seems that I am the winner—
the one who was never found.

Franz Josef Haydn (1732-1809), Quartet in E-flat Major, Op. 33, No. 2, "The Joke"

FLIGHT[10]

Five Tibetan nuns traverse
the peaks and valleys
of the Himalayas,
their footprints
leaving small indentations
in the landscape
of their homeland.

Their maroon robes,
ragged and damp,
drag down their spirits
as they trudge
toward the border.
Om Mani Peme Hung

Snow is white.
Silence is a cloud
released from despair.
There is nothing
to hold onto but belief.
Om Mani Peme Hung

Frost numbs their fingers.
Shaven heads glow
beneath the Hunger Moon.
Om Mani Peme Hung

The refugees rest
in a mountain hut.
Handfuls of *tsampa*.
Click, click, click
of prayer beads.
Om Mani Peme Hung

A Tibetan hare
shows them the way
across the final pass,
strips of white *khata*
wound tightly
around their knuckles.
Om Mani Peme Hung

Crossing the border
into the village of Dharamsala,
they unbind their hands
to present prayer scarves
to their spiritual leader.
Om Mani Peme Hung

Om Mani Peme Hung: Tibetan Buddhist mantra meaning "Behold the jewel in the lotus!"
tsampa: roasted barley flour, the Tibetan staple food
khata: traditional ceremonial scarf presented to a host

Sheila Silver's "The Tale of the White Rooster"

SUSTENANCE[11]

The housekeeper smuggles in food, tucked inside
her winter coat, to feed the composer's family.
Loaves of bread lodge inside the sleeves. Potatoes
bulge like tumors in her pockets. Pinned to the lining,
sackcloth bags of turnips, beets, rutabagas.

The flat is cold. Ants scurry for warmth beneath
the threadbare carpet. Roaches lie in wait for crumbs.
The family huddles around a stove lit by pages
of sheet music. Terror courses through their veins.
We will live.   We will live.   We will live.

Morning. A Siberian weasel waits in the snow
outside their window. Faint hum of his fur.
Dry aftertaste of last night's dream.
The vodka bottle is empty.

Dmitri Shostakovich, Quartet No. 10 in A-flat Major, Op. 118

PURGE

afternoon light disappears
gradual as a kiss between new lovers
reluctant to part

square-heeled boots
clatter on cobblestones
steel-gray uniforms

gunmetal cylinders
point skyward—no
bird sound

just the squeal of bats
spiraling in for the kill
their ink-black wings

    run, run, run, run, run

a girl escapes her pursuers
red streak of her dress
a flag, a badge, a bandage

behind the door
fear trembles
in a trench coat

    knock, knock, knock

dishes shatter, dust spews
from beneath the armoire
all is lost—he has been found

the old woman
stands at the kitchen sink
twisting a dishrag in her hands

stench of cabbage
taste of blood
she bites her lip hard

winter chill
breaks through
the lace curtains

Dmitri Shostokovich (1906-1975), Quartet No. 8 in C minor, Op. 1

MESTO[12]

Dank cave in a foreign land.
A woman sits surrounded
by a circle of stones
to protect her
from night creatures
that crawl and fly.

Day and night, night and day
measured by the stitches
she unravels from a sweater
left by her husband—taken away
how many months ago?

Every day she knits it back together.
The smell of her beloved is fading.
Demon bats sweep down—seize
bits of yarn in their hooked claws.

Nazis strut by—
their staccato words
streaks of lightning
that crack through
the cavity
of her hideaway.

A distant cello
resounds in her ears,
then nails scratching
on dry walls.
A disturbing
dissonance.

The woman stumbles out
into spring sunlight.
Wildflowers are blooming.
Grass is cool and fragrant.

She drapes skeins of yarn
across her swollen belly.
How sweet the lark's song.
How slowly the heart beats at the end.

Mesto: Italian for "sad" and "sorrowful"
Bela Bartok (1881-1945), String Quartet No. 6 composed in Budapest

STREET TALK

Juvies bang on garbage cans with sticks,
baseball bats, and discarded beer bottles
that shatter into a trash pile of notes.

Tykes spin their tricycle wheels—
sound of playing cards
clipped to the spokes.

Trucks rumble by,
barrels of gasoline
bouncing
on their corrugated beds.

Propped up
against a brick wall
a deaf mute—
his outstretched hand.

Steve Reich (1938 -), Mallet Quartet

BENT[13]
    (in eight movements)

1.
Wordsworth's blades of grass
bent down
by a wounded deer

2.
opposite of straight
the useless nail, hunchback
unable to see the sky

3.
arc of arthritic fingers
claws of raccoons, the warped
pendulum that stops time

4.
bend over backwards—
still you cannot
please everyone

5.
lost in the forest
a fugitive bends
to drink the moon

6.
rules bent like barbed wire
how to bend the truth
to stay alive

7.
stoop to the task
of polishing the boots
that kick you

8.
walk to your death
wearing a pink triangle
 zig
  zag
   zig
zag

Philip Glass (1937 –   ), Suite for String Quartet from the film *Bent*

DEATH IS A BUTTERFLY[14]

that lands on her shoulder. Its delicate wings,
a pool of color that seeps into the maiden's
skin through the silk threads of her gown.

Joyful at being chosen, she unties
her bonnet and tosses it into the air.
Her small dog chases the ribbon,
trickling like water
across the garden.

A thrumming from the butterfly.
Death is becoming impatient.
The maiden feels its breath
on her slender white neck,
its exhalation of clover.

Lepidoptera lifts the maiden
by her ringlets, her body light
and willing as mist.

She rises toward the light,
full flounced, singing a single note
of farewell to her little dog
who is chewing on the ribbon
of her abandoned bonnet.

Daniel Kellogg (1976 -), "Soft Sleep Shall Contain You"

AN ARGENTINE GAUCHO[15]

chases his herd across the pampas
   bola swinging in the air
      closer, closer

hooves, dust, grunt of steeds
   crack of cords
      against the bull's hind legs.

Entangled—
   the beast lurches and falls.

After the roundup and mugs of rum,
   two gauchos face off
      to dance a malambo.

Boot heels
   stomp the ground like hooves
      of agitated bulls.

A guitar accelerates
   its frenzied throb.

The opponents eye each other
   like roosters in a cockfight,
      every spin a confrontation

while their paramours
   lounge on the veranda
      at sunset

shawls draped loosely
   around their shoulders
      sipping bittersweet Amaros.

Alberto Ginastera, Quartet No. 1, Op. 20

THE OFFERING

Jeromita's kitchen
smells of cinnamon
and fresh-cut apples.

Wiping her hands on a towel,
she opens the screen door.
Chickens squawk and scatter.

Heat wilts the bougainvillea—
mutes the squeak
of the garden gate.

Lugubrious strumming
from an unshaven guitar player
on Jeromita's front porch.

The brown eggs
she hands him
are warm as skin.

Carlos Guastavino (1912-2000), Las Presencias No. 6, "Jeromita Linares"

ESCAPADES[16]

Swashbuckling scalawags, marauding pirates,
pace the treasure ship in leather pants,
bandanas, and blood-red sashes.

Bach, too, strides the deck with gashes
in his doublet from close escapes
on the high Baroque seas.

And there's that rascal Telemann,
who stole from poor gypsies
and sold to the wealthy.

Tonight the troupe from Red Priest
mount their steeds and prance
through fields, trampling
the seeds of next year's crops.

Under the canopy of darkness,
the rogue quartet moves north,
past windows where tight-lipped
ladies in hoop skirts hover
at the harpsichord,
their bodices heaving
to the gypsy dance.

Horses escape
from their tethers,
their manes lit
by summer stars.

Selected pieces played by Red Priest.

SOUNDS FROM A YAO VILLAGE

A woman   sits by the window   weaving
   her shuttle   moving   back and forth
      marks the passage   of morning hours.

In the forest   hack
   of the woodcutter's   axe
      its handle hewn   from the wood
        that it has   sundered.

The shepherd boy
    sits   beneath   a cypress
       strumming   his zither.

A young girl   washes her robes
   in the river   waterfall sound
      and a distant   cuckoo.

Fragrance
   of honeysuckle
     chittering   sparrows
       still water   runs   deep
         and   soundless.

Selections from Yi-Wen Jiang's "China Song"

I WANT TO LIVE MY LIFE IN A ROTHKO PAINTING

like ocher, settling lightly upon brown earth
seeded with light. Like aquamarine blue
sinking into a sea of violet.

I will live in an orange house with a yellow roof
and peach trees growing in the orchard. Hang
my red slip on a clothesline at twilight.

I will lick rectangles of color papering my walls,
layers of tangerine and sweet vanilla. Burn
my throat on strips of alizarin red.

I will drink from a black cup that never empties.
Sit in front of a fire and breathe in the coal-gray
scent of charcoal as flames burn through it.

I will slip inside the caress of a beige blanket,
curl up on saffron pillows, and dream of
translucent bottles holding no fragrance.

Inside the Rothko painting, I will listen
to maroon walls sing beneath the blackest
windows while I watch the sun set
behind my two-dimensional life.

Franz Joseph Haydn, Quartet in B-flat Major, Op. 76, No. 4, "Sunrise"

GREAT AUNT REGINA OF LYSKI

Great Aunt Regina has a bathtub in the corner
of her living room, concealed behind a curtain.

Great Aunt Regina has ripe tomatoes on a sideboard
and vodka she serves us in small crystal glasses.

Great Aunt Regina has relatives. Ah, so many sons
and daughters and cousins and in-laws who all come

to meet her great niece with blonde hair and blue eyes—
the American granddaughter of her eldest sister, Rozalia

who left the garment factory at sixteen and traveled alone
on a ship to the New World before Regina was born.

Great Aunt Regina sits us all down at the table—
shows us photographs of her dead husband and then

her son lying in the casket dressed in his Sunday suit.
Another round of vodka. *Nostrovia!*

Everyone cries. Everyone laughs. We all talk at once.
The party goes on and on and on.

A full moon shines down on the village of Lyski,
on my Polish family that I am seeing for the first time

with my grandmother's eyes.

Sulkhan Zinzadze, Georgian Folk Suite

ONE LAST SCHERZO

Wind settles and tucks itself
inside the petals of white tulips
as the sun sinks behind hills.

Bees buzz one last scherzo
before they succumb
to the honeyed dusk.

An army of ants terminates
its march at the end
of the cracked sidewalk.

Grasshoppers buzz and flick
themselves into dark grasses
where they kneel in repose.

Stars, hidden behind a curtain
of clouds all day, begin their display
falling to earth as fireflies.

Hairy white legs, goat-footed
and cocky, bowlegged and bawdy.
Where did this satyr come from?

Bearded like a Billy Goat Gruff,
he plays his flute song, wanton
as weeds on a midsummer's night.

scherzo: rapid, playful, or humorous movement
Felix Mendelssohn, Octet for Strings in E-flat Major, Op. 20

Notes

1. Brahms wrote this first sextet at age twenty-seven. In a letter to Clara Schumann, which accompanied the manuscript, he told her to "burn the trash" rather than bother to return it. When writing "Rendezvous", I envisioned a reunion between Brahms and his beloved friend, Clara.

2. In "A Garret in Krakow", I pictured Penderecki seated at his desk, much as a writer would, waiting for inspiration. Krakow is the birthplace of my paternal grandparents, and I've visited several times.

3. Janácek began his music studies as a choirboy in a monastery in Moravia (now the Czech Republic). "Intimate Letters" refers to the more than 700 letters he wrote to his muse, Kamila Stösslová, though his love was not reciprocated. "Feelings are so powerful that the music hides behind them—a great love and a weak composition, but I want this to be a great love and a great composition." (from program notes by Joan Rogers)

4. In his twenties, Mozart suffered from the burden of his father's criticism and his neediness. Leopold also suggested that Mozart write chamber pieces that were "short, easy, and popular". To preserve his aesthetic sensibility and peace of mind, Mozart escaped to Vienna. (from program notes by Joan Rogers)

5. This quartet is sometimes called the Komplimentier Quartett due to the courtly, hat-doffing figures in the opening movement. The dialogue develops into a charming, yet ironic, exchange of courtesies to further deepen this comedy of manners. (from program notes by Joan Rogers)

6. Mendelssohn's sister, Fanny, was a musical genius, but was unable to pursue a professional career because of social constraints of the time. She wrote 466 musical compositions, some published under her brother's name. Fanny died of a stroke in 1847 and, six months later, Mendelssohn also suffered a stroke and died.

7 "Serioso" is the shortest and most impassioned of Beethoven's 16 quartets. He'd suffered a separation from a woman friend and was at an impasse in his musical life. In a letter to his friend, George Smart, he said: "The Quartet is written for a small circle of connoisseurs and is never to be performed in public". (from program notes by Susan Halprin)

8. The Calder Quartet performed Jacob ter Veldhuis's Quartet No. 3 ("There must be some way out of here") on March 14, 2011, just three days after the disastrous earthquake, tsunami, and nuclear meltdown in Fukushima, Japan.

9. In the first movement of this piece about 9/11, Steve Reich uses warning beeps that a phone makes when it's off the hook, as well as archived voices from traffic controllers. The second movement uses recordings made of neighborhood residents, and the third, voices of neighbors who took shifts sitting near the bodies. WTC is also an abbreviation for "World To Come", identifying body parts and reciting Psalms for the dead. (from program notes by the Kronos Quartet)

10. Sheila Silver's "The Tale of the White Rooster" weaves together medieval and contemporary songs exploring universal ideas of spirituality. Five Tibetan Buddhist nuns flee to India. When one is wounded, they take refuge in an abandoned hut and enact a Tibetan folktale to console her. The cantata uses six Tibetan singing bowls, hand percussion, and four treble voices. (from program notes by Tapestry)

11. Although the quartet opens on a subdued theme, I concentrated on the second movement with its sharp, jabbing notes and an agitated piece by the cello. During the pre-concert lecture, I learned that Shostakovich slept with his clothes on in case Stalin's soldiers came to take him away. His courageous housekeeper smuggled in food for the family.

12. The String Quartet No. 6 was composed in Budapest in 1939 as the rise of Fascism in Europe coalesced into the inevitability of war. Bartok made plans to emigrate, but stayed in Hungary due to his mother's serious illness. She died in December, 1939. When writing *Mesto*, I imagined a composer's wife hiding from the Nazis. (from program notes by Joan Rogers)

13. Philip Glass scored sections of the film *Bent* for a string quartet. In *Bent*, the main character, Max, is captured and sent to a Nazi labor camp. On the train, he falls in love with Horst. The title "Bent" refers to a scene of mental and physical torture, which Nazis inflicted on Max for not only being Jewish, but also a homosexual. (from program notes by Richard Guerin)

14. "Soft Sleep Shall Contain You" is a meditation on Schubert's "Death and the Maiden". Death's conversation with the maiden begins and ends quietly, but the middle section reaches a violent dissonance. I focused on death as a pleasant experience (taken away by an ephemeral butterfly), and added a charming, but clueless dog.

15. The first movement contains rocking, galloping rhythms that evoke Argentine gauchos. The second movement has a robust and earthy quality,

and the third is meditative. I rendered these musical movements into three scenes—the roundup, dancing the malambo, and the paramours relaxing on the veranda.

16. Leading musicians of this time were pioneers and adventurers, riding the seas of change with wild abandon. The theme of musical piracy extends from the poaching of themes. Georg Telemann stole the tunes of poor gypsies from Eastern Europe. Antonio Vivaldi, called the Red Priest of Venice, was described as a man with too much mercury in his constitution. The search for music of the past is like a treasure hunt. (from program notes by Piers Adams)

Publications

All the poems in *One Last Scherzo* were posted on the Friends of Chamber Music website for patrons, musicians, and music lovers to enjoy. In addition, the following appeared in concert programs: Concave, For Fanny, *Mesto*, One Last Scherzo, and Vienna Salon.

Czech Nonet featured several poems in their exhibition "Music & Painting" in Prague, The Czech Republic, in 2011.

In 2012, I was interviewed and invited to read a selection of these poems on All Classical radio in Portland, Oregon, streaming to a worldwide audience.

"Purge" is collected in the personal papers of composer George Crumb.

"Inundation" was included in *We Are All Japan* (2013), an anthology to honor the victims of the Fukushima earthquake and tsunami disaster. It also appears in the anthology *Nuclear Impact: Broken Atoms in Our Hands*, Shabda Press, 2017.

"Death is a Butterfly" was displayed as a broadside for a poetry reading at the Pond House in Milwaukie, Oregon, 2011.

"Great Aunt Regina of Lyski" was published in *U.S. Worksheets 1*, 2014

"I Want to Live in a Rothko Painting," was published in *Willawaw Journal*, 2018

www.ingramcontent.com/pod-product-compliance
Lightning Source LLC
LaVergne TN
LVHW041556070426
835507LV00011B/1120